A First-Start Easy Reader

This easy reader contains only 32 different words,
repeated often to help the young reader develop
word recognition and interest in reading.

Basic word list for *Willie the Slowpoke*

is	what	time
it	for	Willie
to	get	breakfast
up	getting	dinner
but	go	school
he	going	home
be	not	meeting
too	will	ready
a	late	tomorrow
on	out	because
the		play

Willie
the Slowpoke

Written by Rose Greydanus

Illustrated by Andrea Eberbach

Troll Associates

Printed in the United States of America.

ISBN 0-89375-294-0

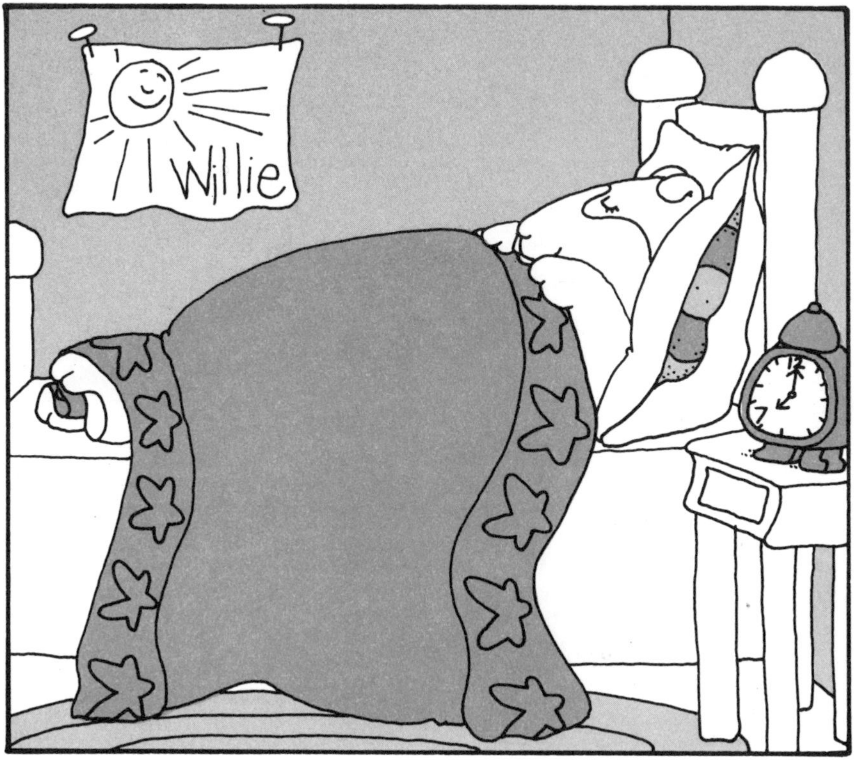
Willie

What time is it?

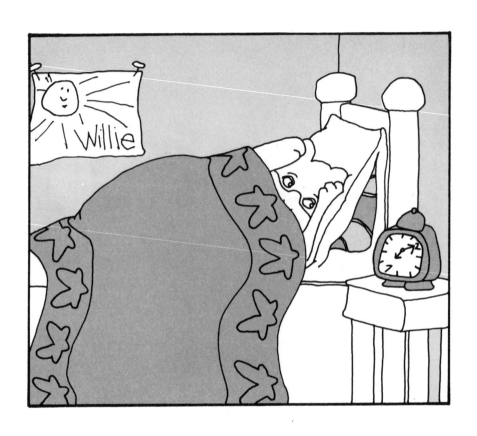

It is time for Willie to get up.

But Willie is not getting up.

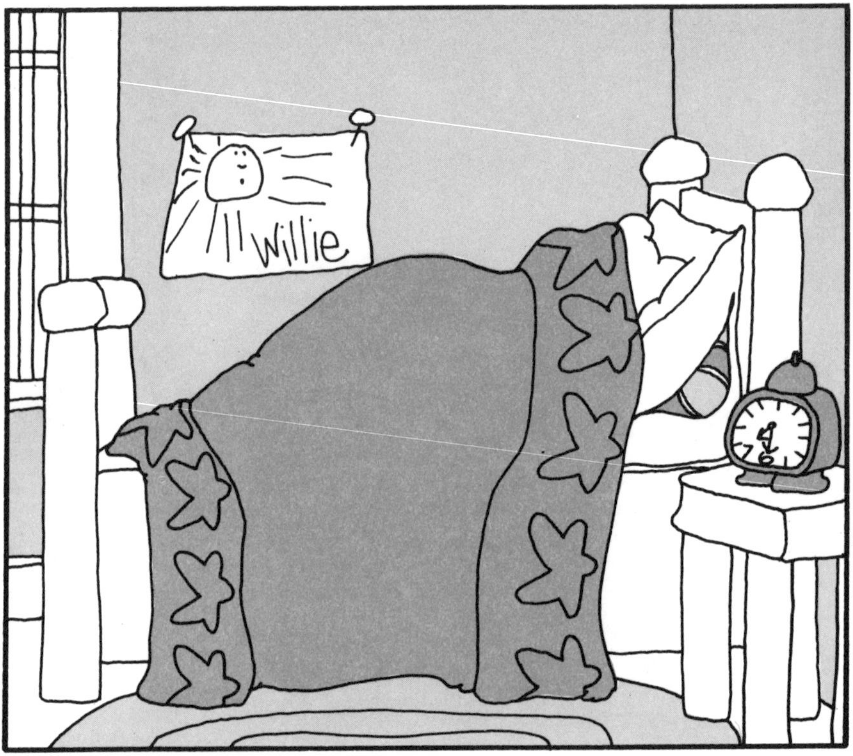
Willie

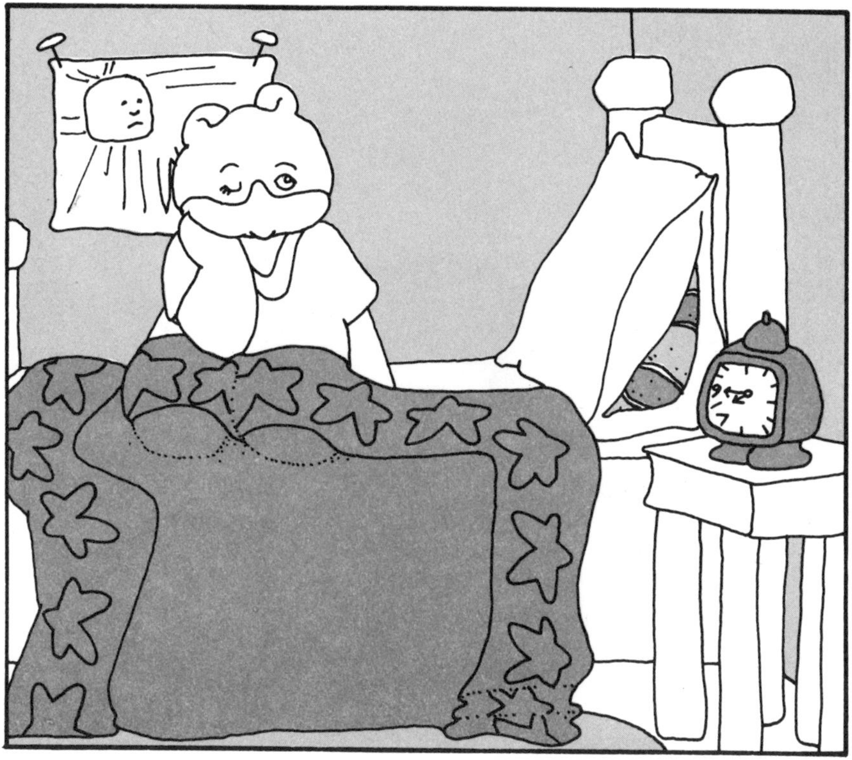

He will be late.

He will be late for breakfast.

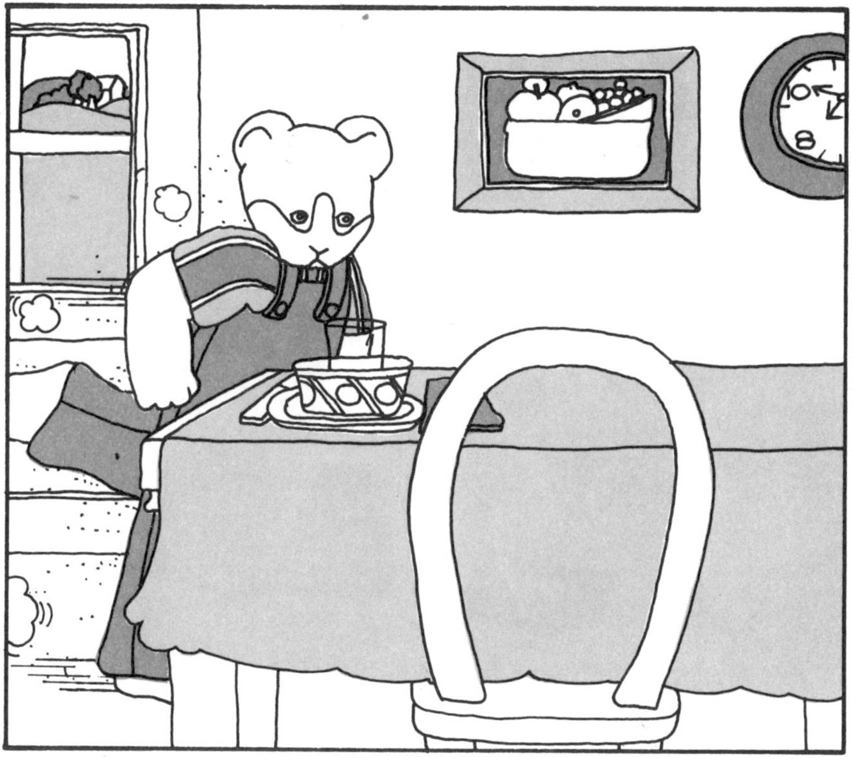

Too late, Willie!

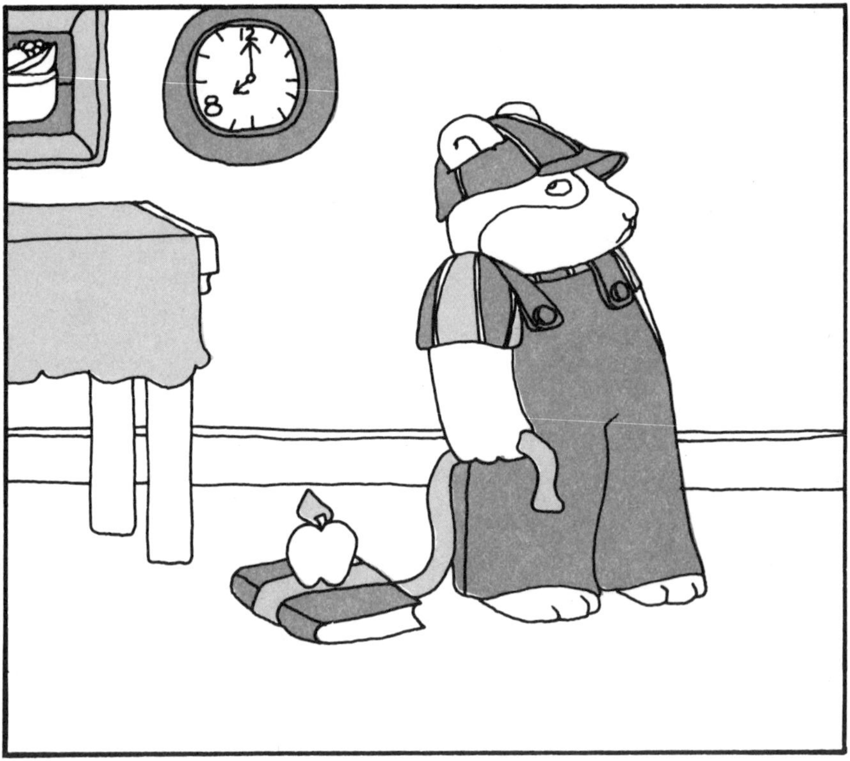

It is time for Willie to go to school.

He will be late for school.

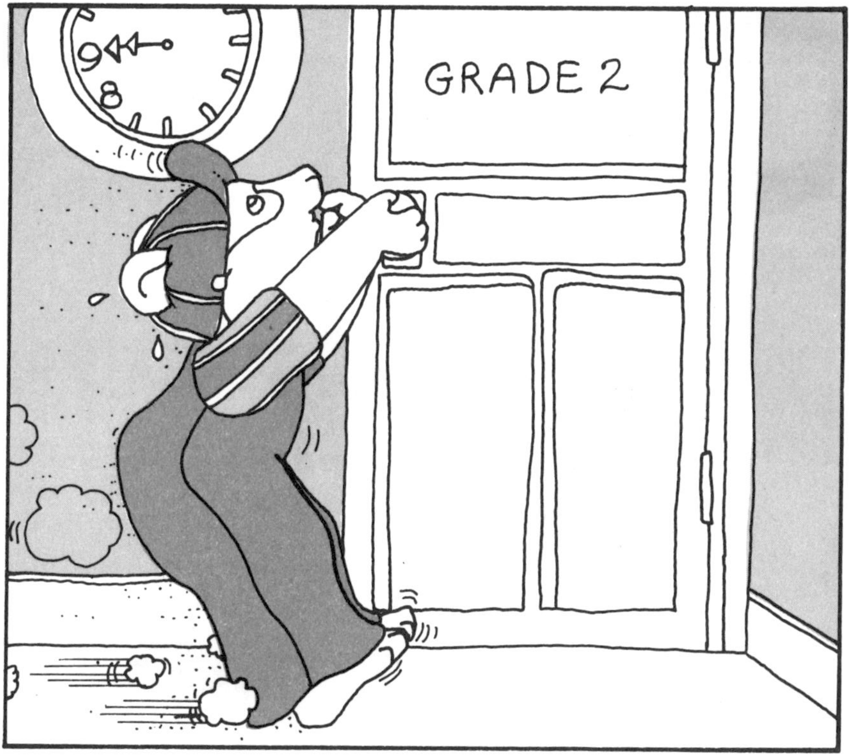
GRADE 2

Too late, Willie!

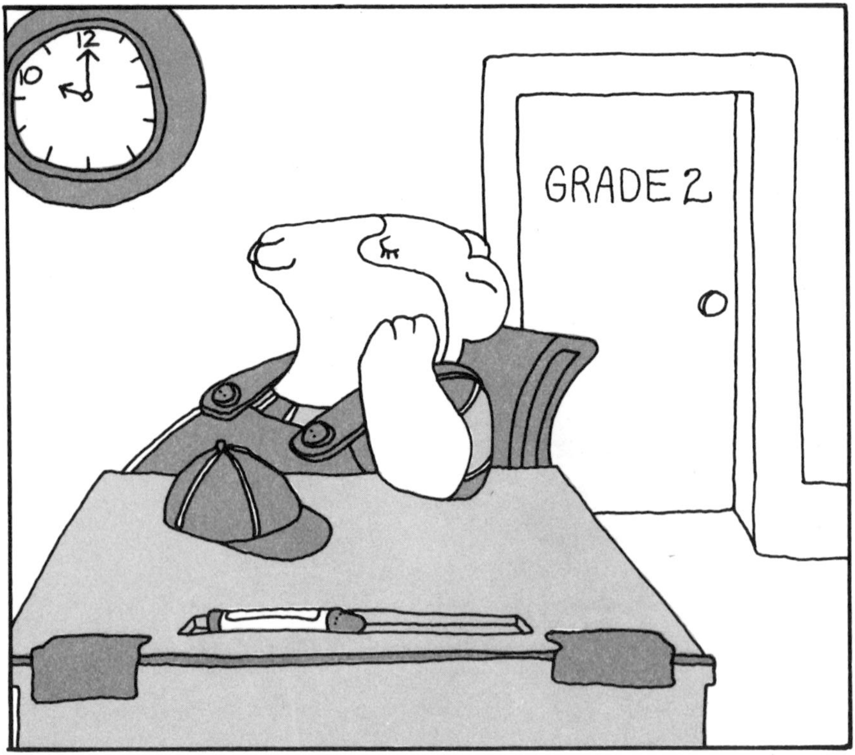
GRADE 2

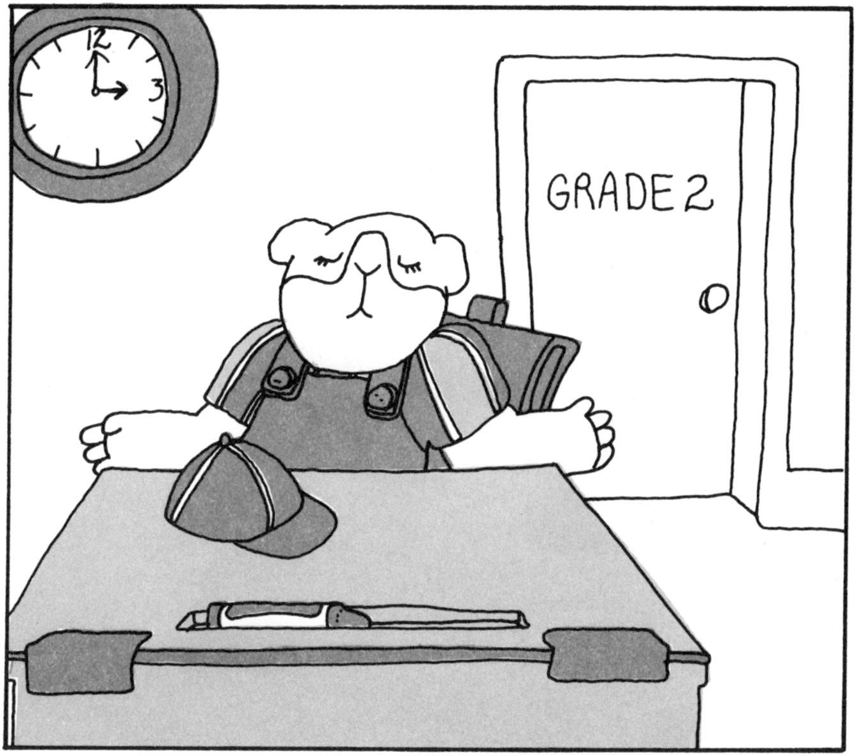
12
3
GRADE 2

What time is it?

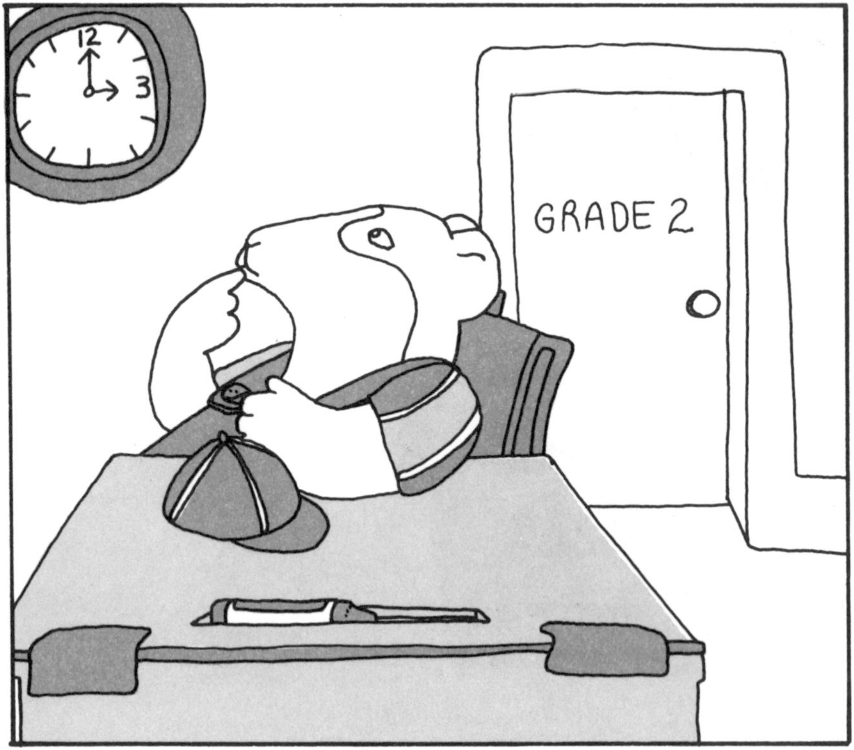
12
3
GRADE 2

It is time to go home.

But Willie is not going home.

Willie will be late for dinner.

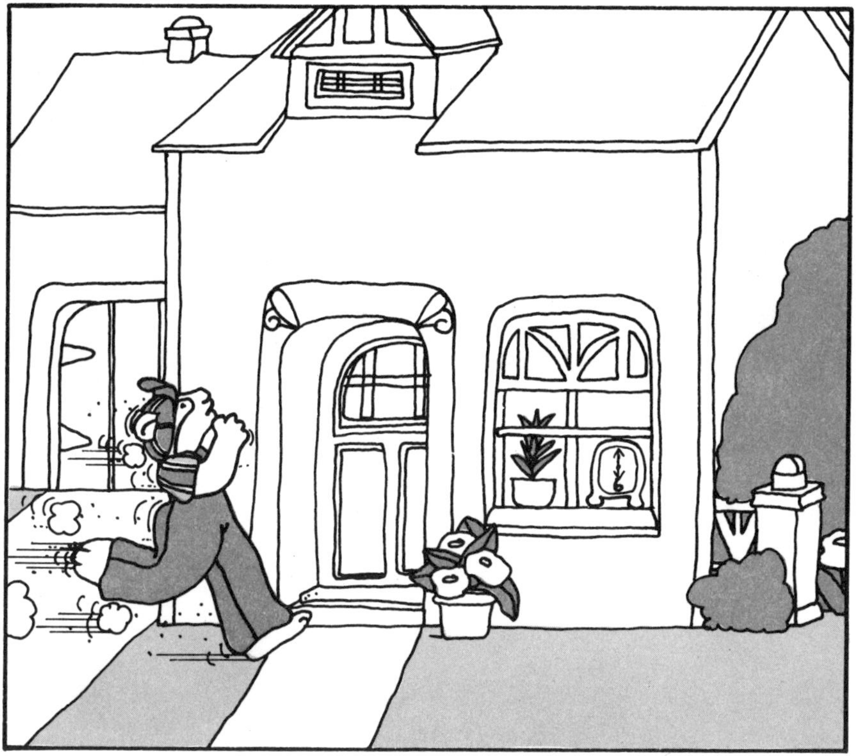

Too late, Willie!

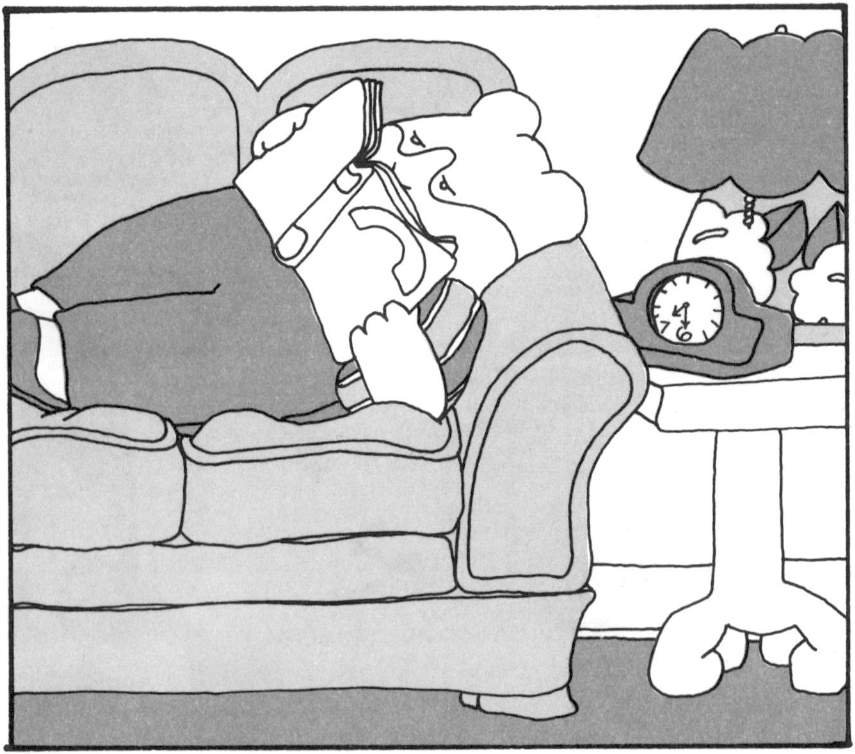

What time is it?

It is time to go to a meeting.

But Willie is not getting ready.

He will be late.

Willie will be late for the meeting.

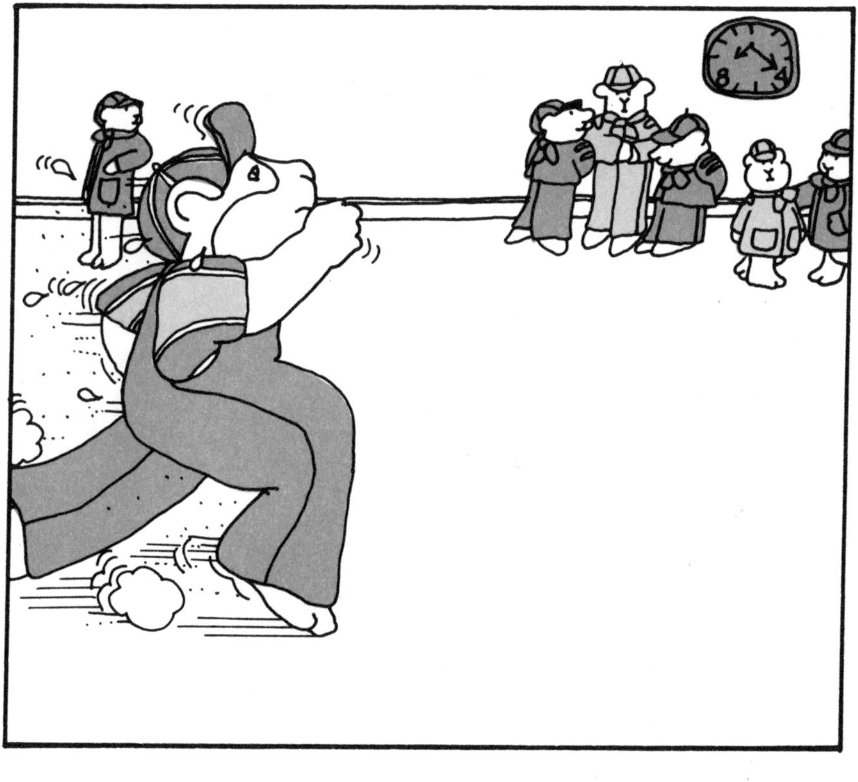

Too late, Willie!

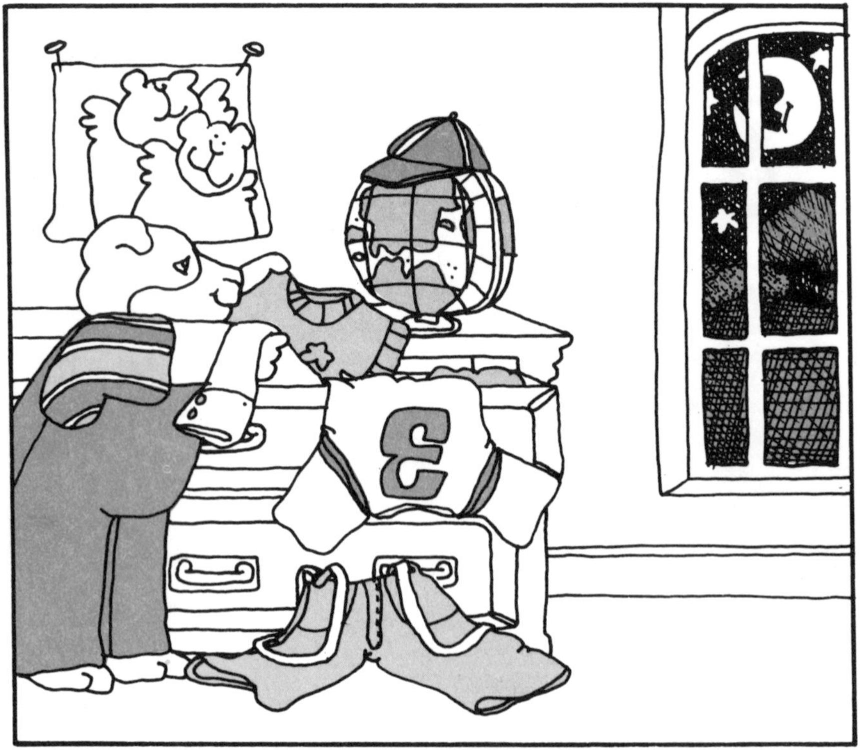

But tomorrow . . . tomorrow . . .

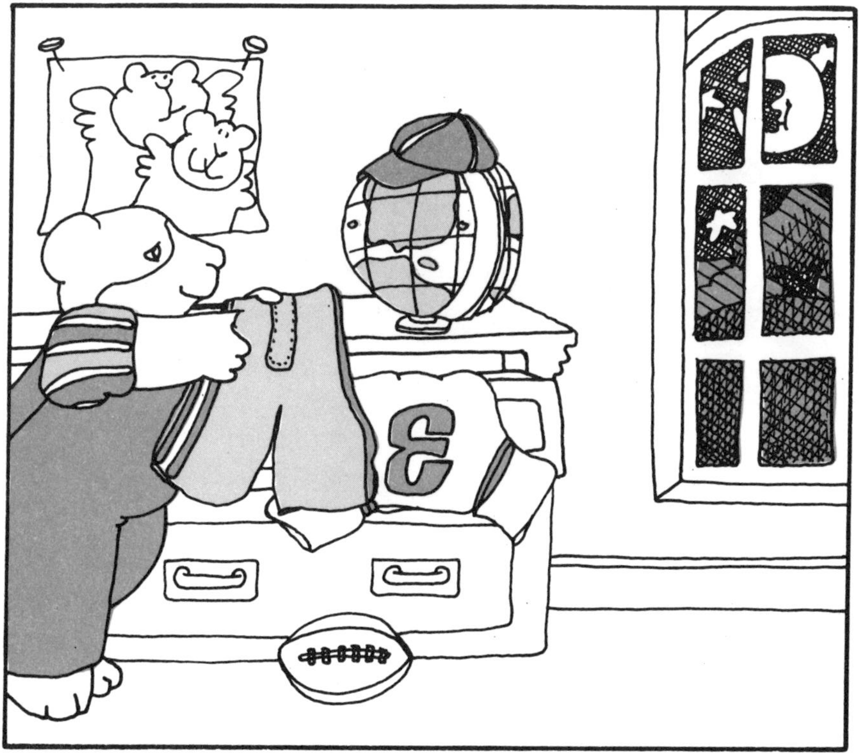

. . . Willie will be ready.

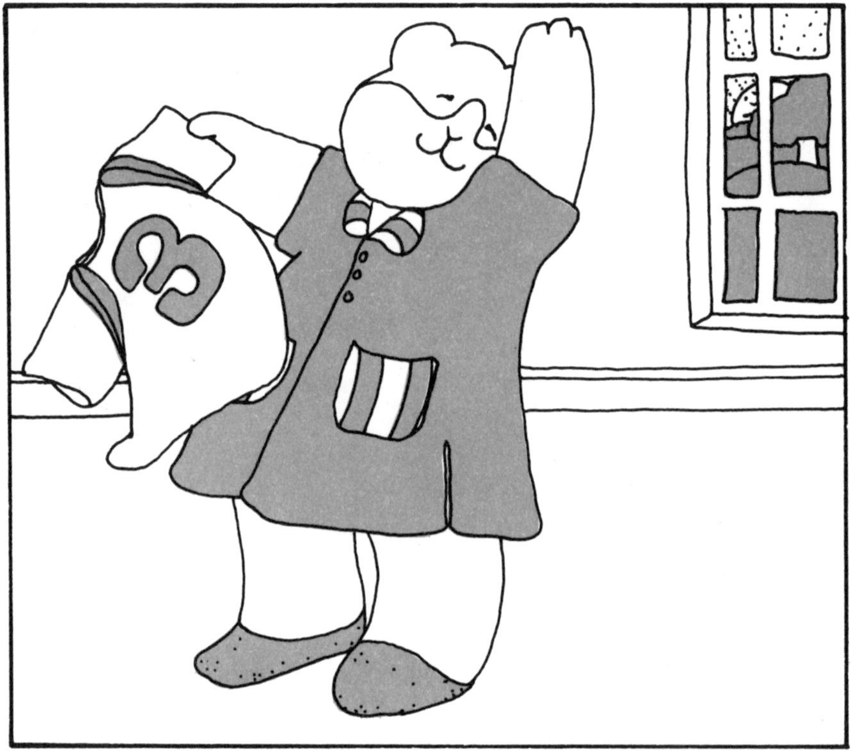

Willie will be on time.

Because Willie is going out to play!